NEW CI
TO MODERNS

MW01091947

FOREWORD

This latest volume in the Music for Millions Series, New Classics to Moderns, brings together 102 pieces from the piano repertoire spanning four centuries, from the early Baroque period through to the work of contemporary composers.

Playing through the book provides a remarkable insight into the progression of piano music and the inexorable musical connections that exist between old and contemporary composers alike, especially in the governance and influence of tonality, a theme which binds the repertory of the book together.

Almost all the selections are in their original form, with a few slightly simplified versions to create a unified standard of difficulty. As with the previous volumes, the pieces are set in chronological order. Marks of phrasing and expression are often editorial additions, especially in earlier music. These signs were added for a quicker, easier understanding of the structure and mood of the compositions thus should be considered as suggestions rather than precise directions. The student should always defer to the judgement of their teacher.

Students, teachers and pianists of all levels will find here a great variety of pieces valuable for study, recital, sight reading, or just relaxing musical entertainment of the highest calibre.

THE PUBLISHER

WISE PUBLICATIONS
PART OF THE MUSIC SALES GROUP
LONDON / NEW YORK / PARIS / SYDNEY / COPENHAGEN / BERLIN / MADRID / HONG KONG / TOKYO

CONTENTS

CONTENTS

Published by
Wise Publications
14-15 Berners Street,
London W1T 3LJ, UK.

Exclusive Distributors:
Music Sales Limited
Distribution Centre, Newmarket Road,
Bury St Edmunds, Suffolk IP33 3YB, UK.
Music Sales Corporation
180 Madison Avenue, 24th Floor,
New York NY 10016, USA.
Music Sales Pty Limited
Level 4, Lisgar House,
30-32 Carrington Street,
Sydney, NSW 2000 Australia.

Order No. AM1004531
ISBN 978-1-78038-483-2

Compiled and edited by Sam Lung and James Welland.
Music engraved and processed by Camden Music Services,
Paul Ewers Music Design, SEL Music Art Ltd and Sam Lung.
Cover designed by Raissa Pardini.

Printed in the EU.

Your Guarantee of Quality
As publishers, we strive to produce every book to the
highest commercial standards.
This book has been carefully designed to minimise awkward
page turns and to make playing from it a real pleasure.
Particular care has been given to specifying acid-free, neutral-sized paper
made from pulps which have not been elemental chlorine bleached.
This pulp is from farmed sustainable forests and was
produced with special regard for the environment.
Throughout, the printing and binding have been planned to
ensure a sturdy, attractive publication which should give years of enjoyment.
If your copy fails to meet our high standards,
please inform us and we will gladly replace it.

www.musicsales.com

Sarabande

Johann Jakob Froberger
1616–1667

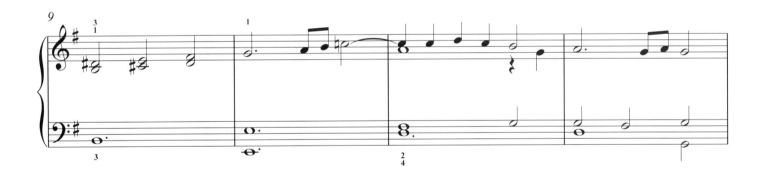

Gavotte

Daniel Speer
1636–1709

Bourrée

Robert de Visée
*c.*1655–1733

Air in D Minor

Henry Purcell
1659–1695

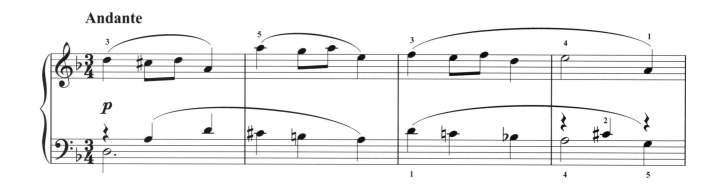

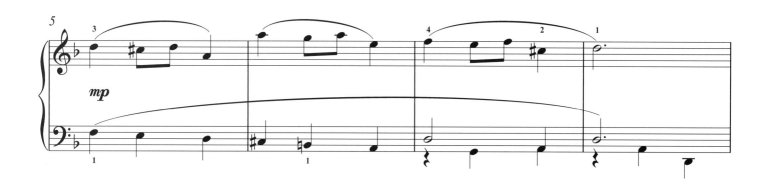

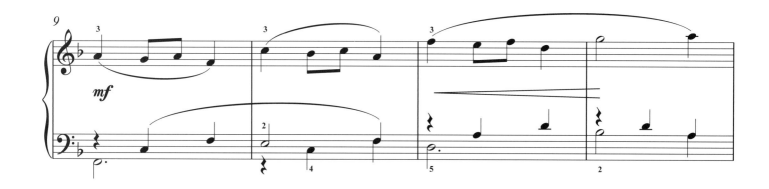

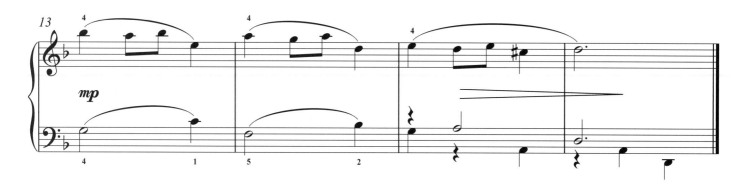

Arioso

Alessandro Scarlatti
1660–1725

Le Petit-Rien

No.4 *from* 5 Pièces de Clavecin

François Couperin
1668–1733

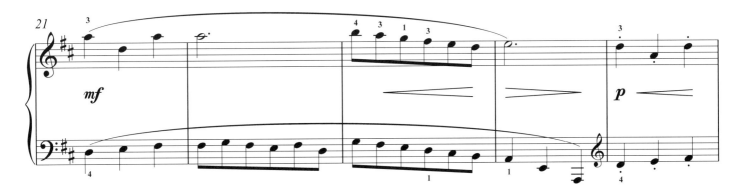

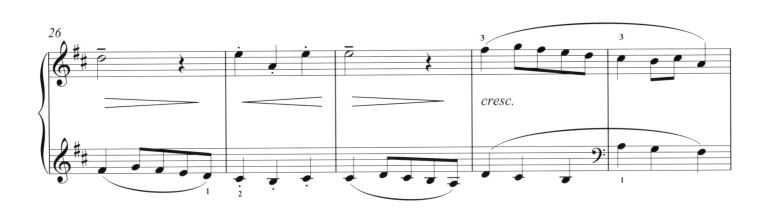

poco rit.

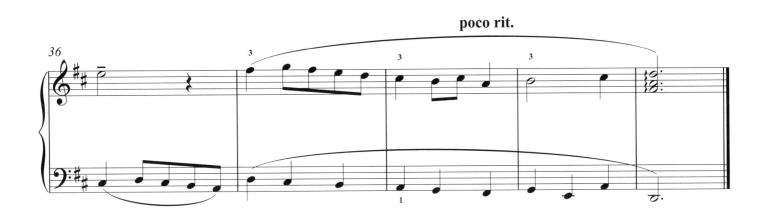

Prélude non mesuré

Gaspard Le Roux
1660–1707

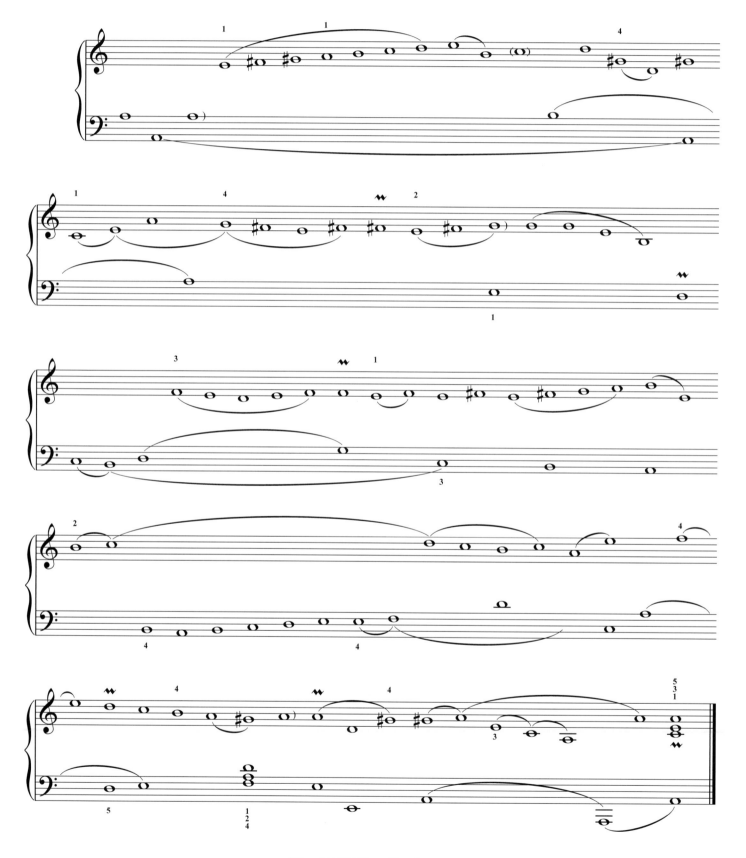

King William's March

Jeremiah Clarke
1674–1707

Autumn

from The Four Seasons

Antonio Vivaldi
1678–1741

Allegro

dim.

Menuet

William Croft
1678–1727

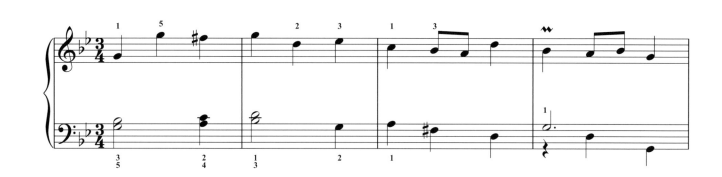

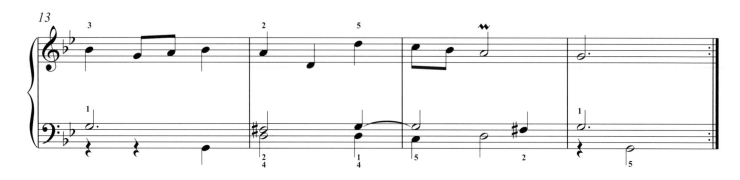

Danse Galante

Georg Philipp Telemann
1681–1767

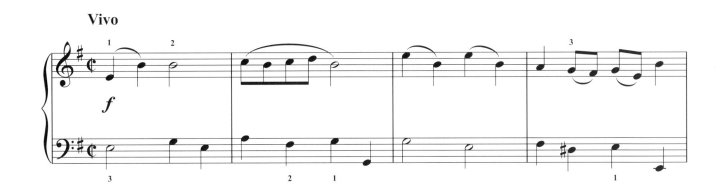

Bourrée

Christophe Graupner
1683–1760

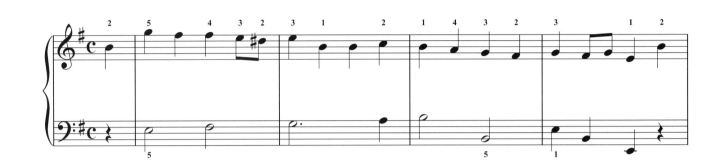

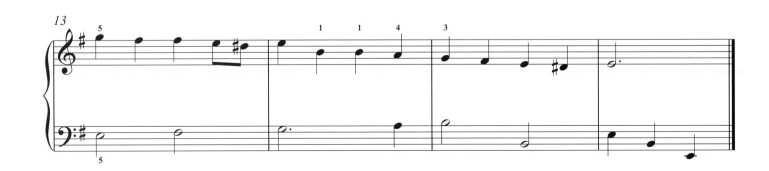

Bourée

from Suite in E Minor, BWV 996

Johann Sebastian Bach
1685–1750

Minuet in G Major

Johann Sebastian Bach
1685–1750

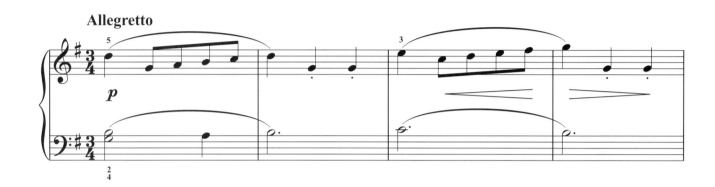

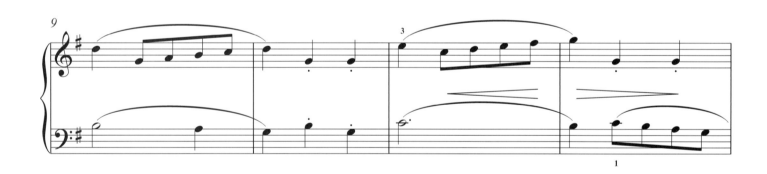

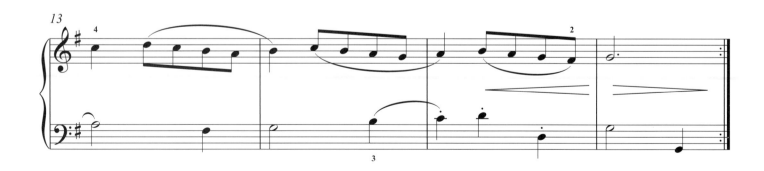

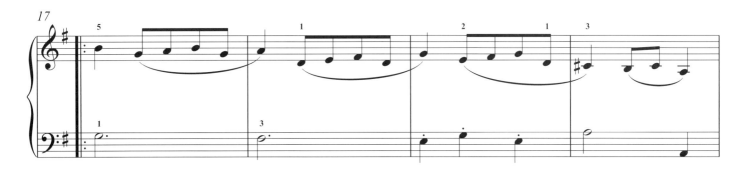

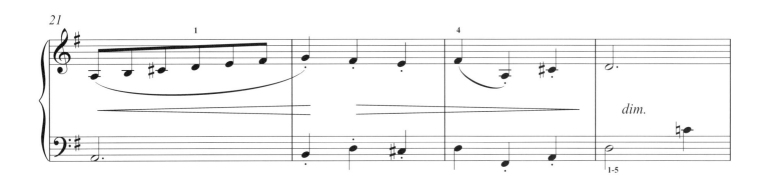

Prelude No.1 in C Major

Johann Sebastian Bach
1685–1750

Moderato e legato

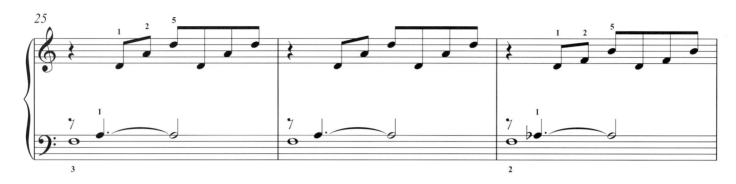

Gavotte

George Frideric Handel
1685–1759

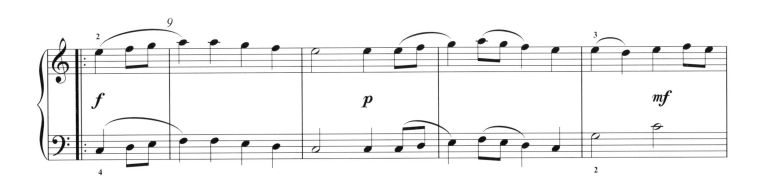

Sarabande in D Minor

George Frideric Handel
1685–1759

Air

Wilhelm Friedemann Bach
1710–1784

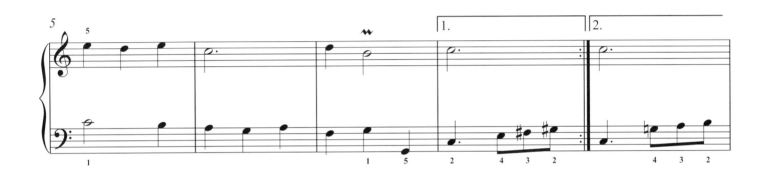

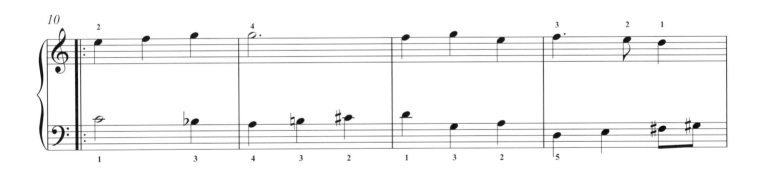

Entrée

Leopold Mozart
1719–1787

Minuet No.3

from 10 Minuets, Hob.IX:22

Joseph Haydn
1732–1809

Surprise Symphony

Theme

Joseph Haydn
1732–1809

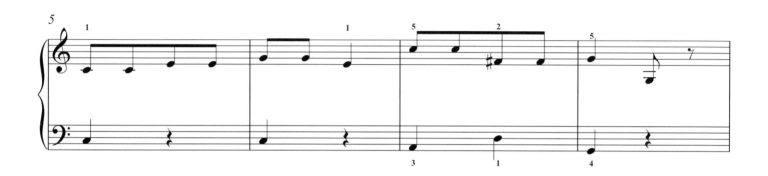

Quadrille

Joseph Haydn
1732–1809

Allegretto

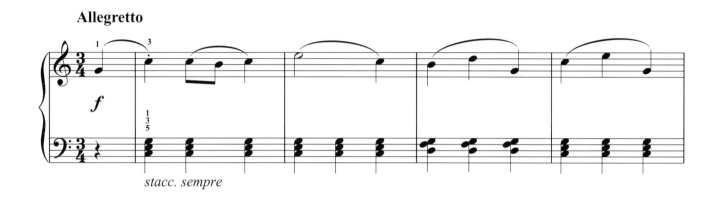

Fanfare Minuet

William Duncombe
1738–1818

Minuetto

Lesson 8 *from* Guida di musica, Op.37

James Hook
1746–1827

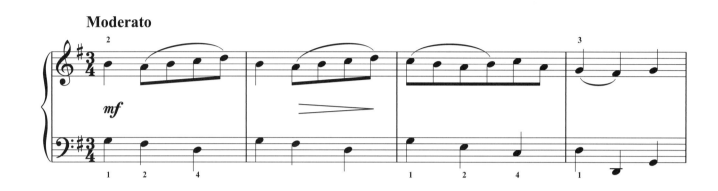

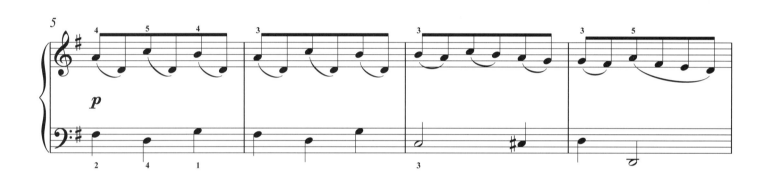

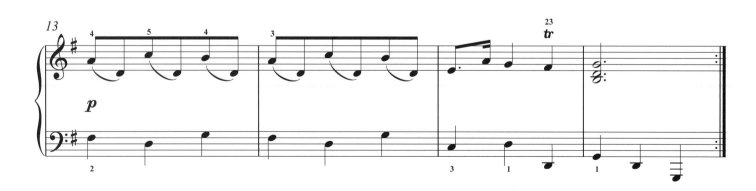

Gavotta

James Hook
1746–1827

Minuet, K.15c

No.29 *from* The London Sketchbook

Wolfgang Amadeus Mozart
1756–1791

Minuet, K.15pp

No.64 *from* The London Sketchbook

Wolfgang Amadeus Mozart
1756–1791

Là ci darem la mano

from Don Giovanni

Wolfgang Amadeus Mozart
1756–1791

Moderato

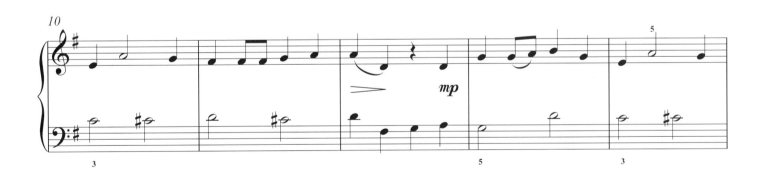

Clarinet Concerto

Adagio

Wolfgang Amadeus Mozart
1756–1791

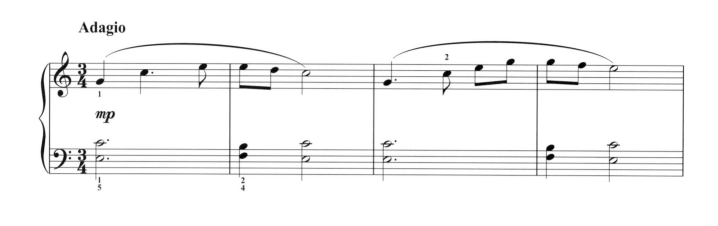

Miniature Rondo

No.22 *from* 120 Pieces For Aspiring Pianists

Daniel Gottlob Türk
1756–1813

Country Dance in D Minor, WoO.15

Ludwig van Beethoven
1770–1827

Russian Folk Song

Ludwig van Beethoven
1770–1827

Für Elise

Ludwig van Beethoven
1770–1827

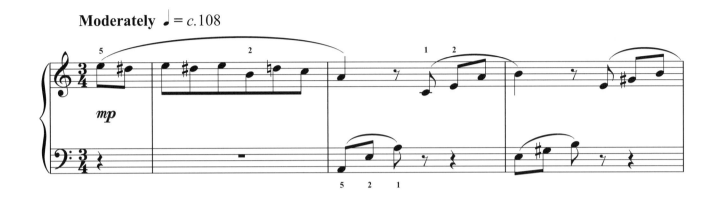

Ecossaise

Johann Nepomuk Hummel
1778–1837

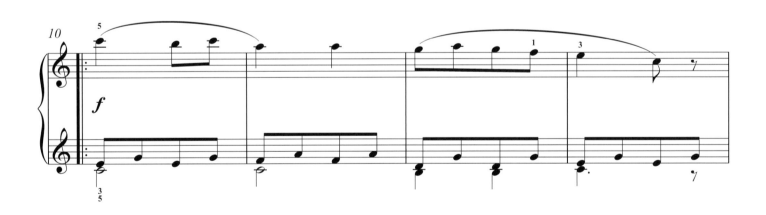

Walking

Anton Diabelli
1781–1858

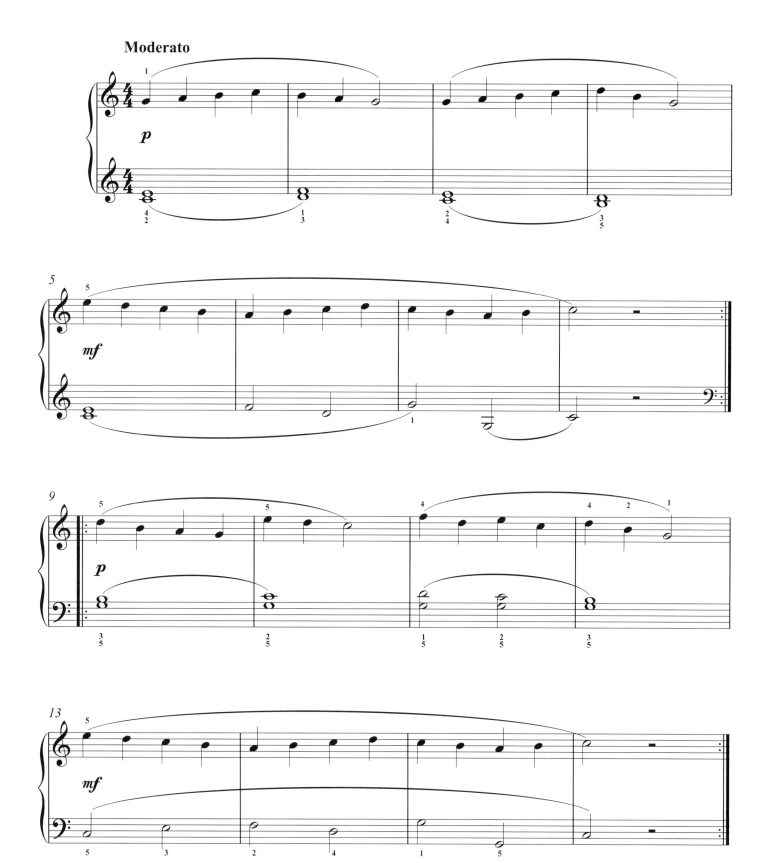

Bagatelle

Johann Nepomuk Hummel
1778–1837

Ländler

No.2 *from* Four Ländlers

Franz Schubert
1791–1828

Ecossaise No.5

from Eight Ecossaises, D.977

Franz Schubert
1791–1828

Nocturne in E♭

Op. 9, No. 2

Frédéric Chopin
1810–1849

52

William Tell Overture

Gioachino Rossini
1792–1868

Bright

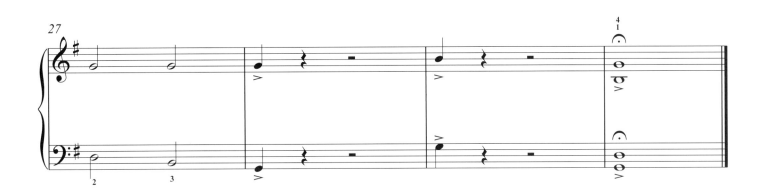

Melody

No.1 *from* Album For The Young, Op.68

Robert Schumann
1810–1856

Little Piece

No.5 *from* Album For The Young, Op.68

Robert Schumann
1810–1856

The Italian Pipers

Charles Gounod
1818–1894

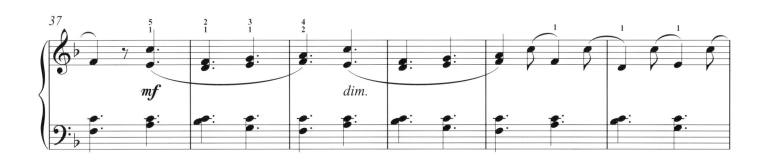

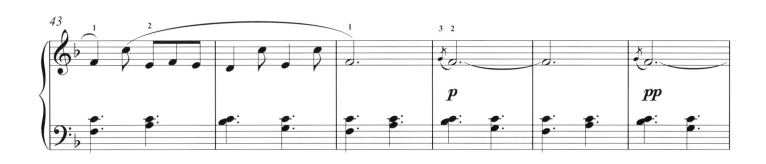

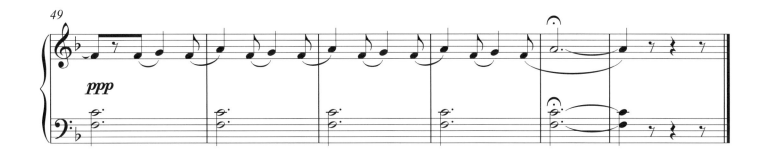

Puppet's Complaint

César Franck
1822–1890

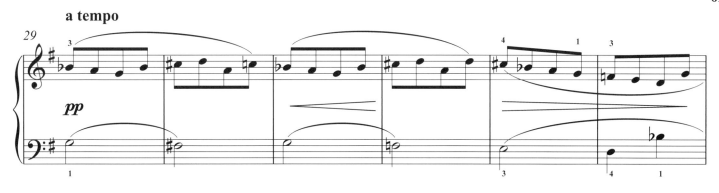

a tempo

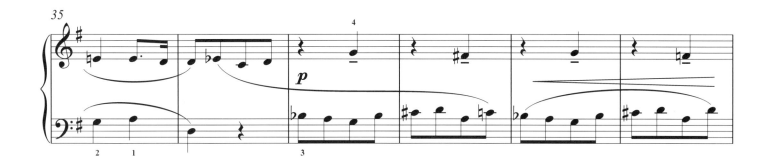

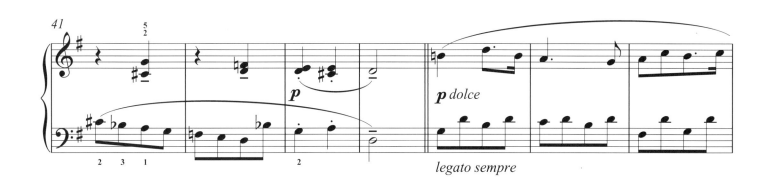

Panis Angelicus

César Franck
1822–1890

Poco lento

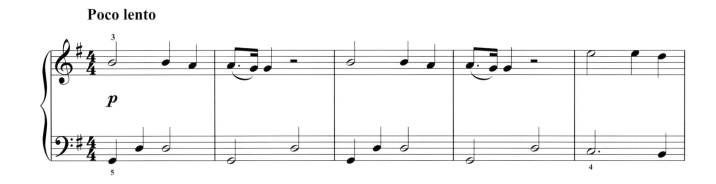

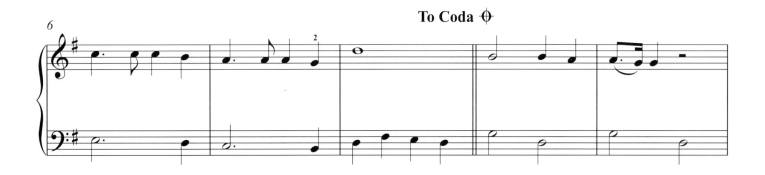

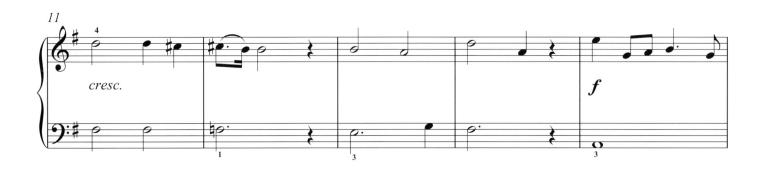

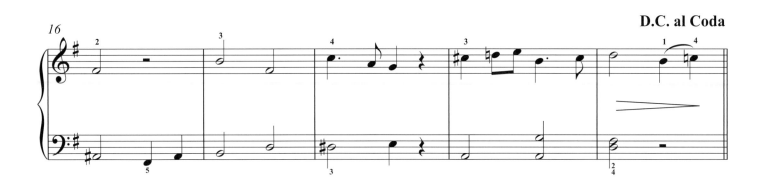

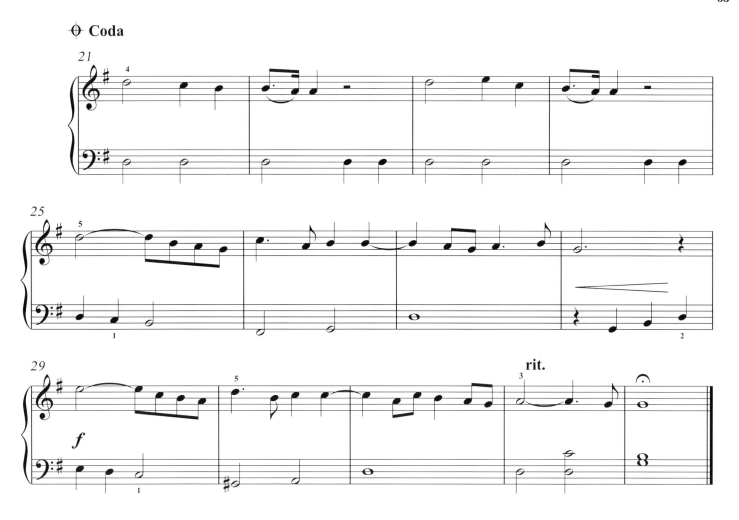

The Hunter's Song

No.10 from The First Lessons, Op.117

Cornelius Gurlitt
1820–1901

The Can-Can

from Orpheus In The Underworld

Jacques Offenbach
1819–1880

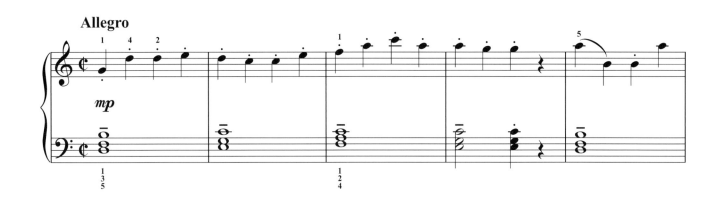

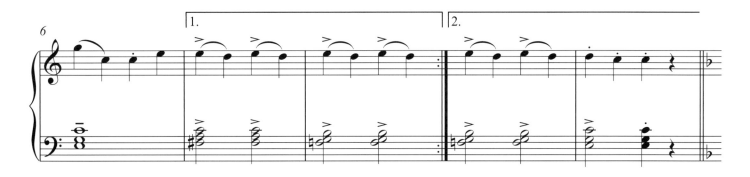

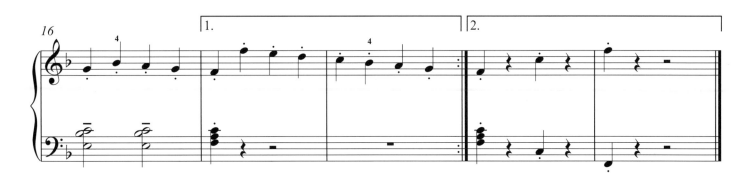

Song Without Words

Carl Reinecke
1824–1910

Cradle Song

No.4 *from* 5 Lieder, Op.49

Johannes Brahms
1833–1897

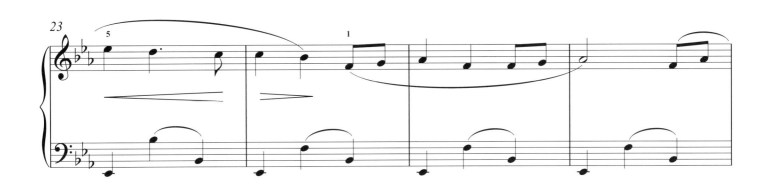

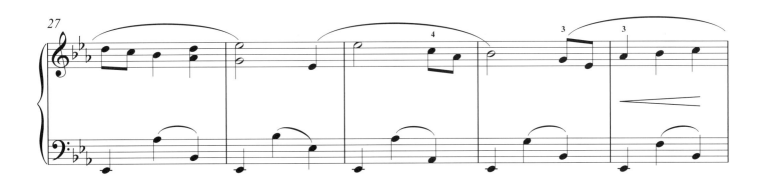

dim. e rall. al fine

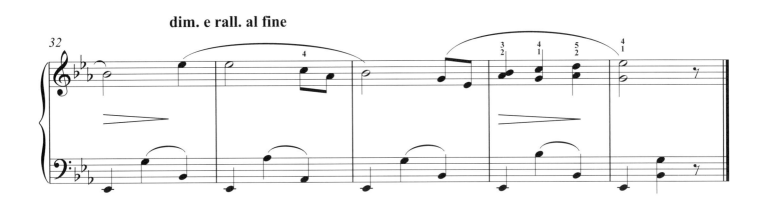

Hungarian Dance No.5

Johannes Brahms
1833–1897

To Begin With

No.1 from Little Piano Pieces, Op.81

Peter Nicolai von Wilm
1834–1911

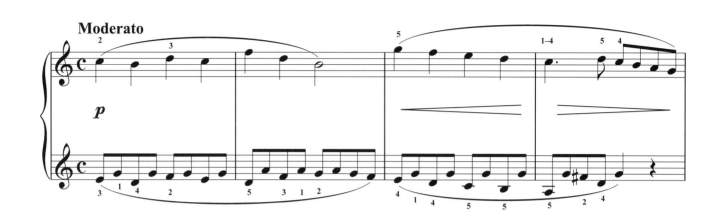

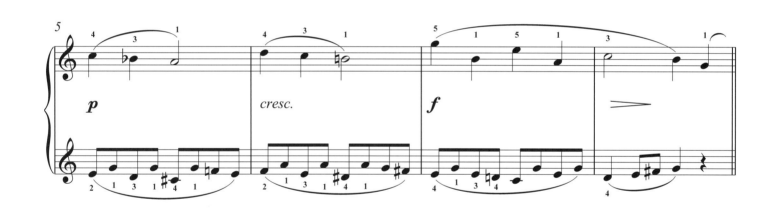

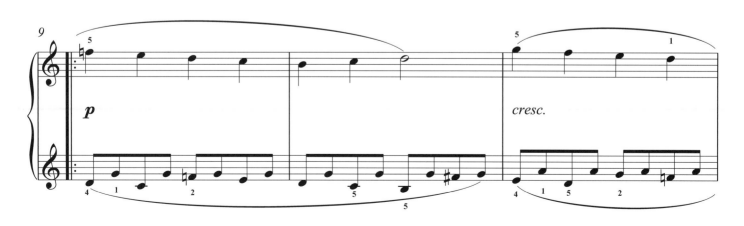

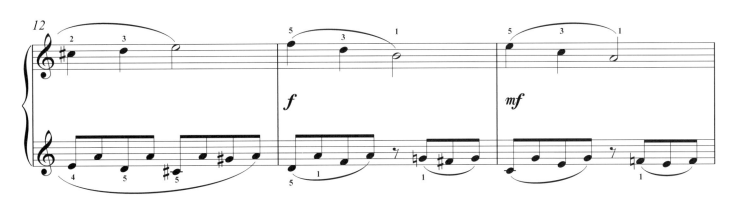

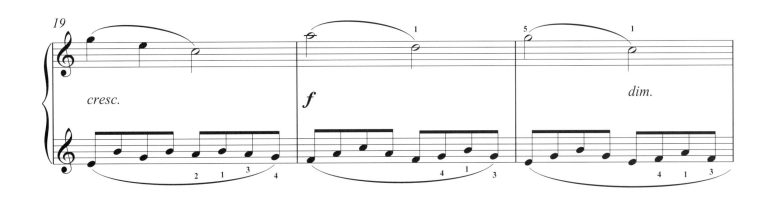

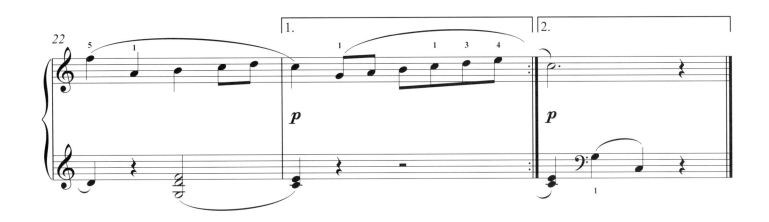

Farandole

from L'Arlésienne Suite

Georges Bizet
1838–1875

Cradle Song

Eduard Horak
1838–1893

The Swan

from Carnival Of The Animals

Camille Saint-Saëns
1835–1921

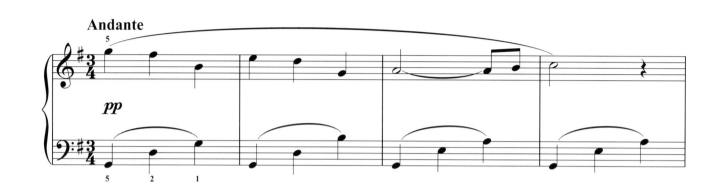

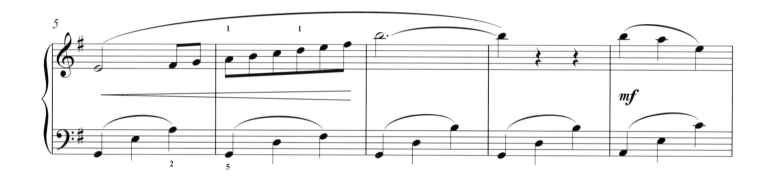

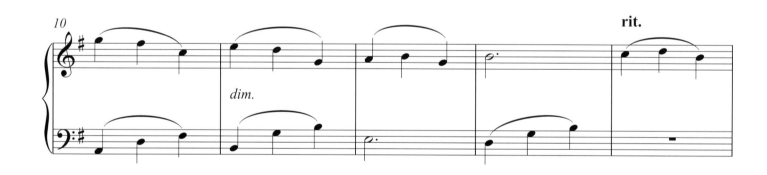

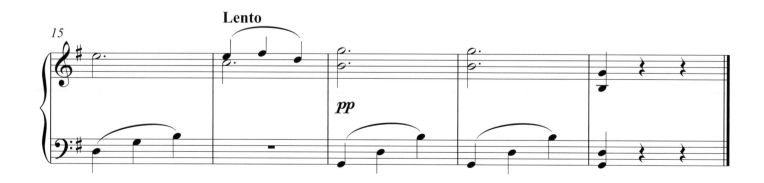

Dance Of The Sugar Plum Fairy

from The Nutcracker Suite

Pyotr Ilyich Tchaikovsky
1840–1893

Largo

from Symphony No. 9 'From The New World'

Antonín Dvořák
1841–1904

Largo

Brave Knight

Moritz Vogel
1846–1922

Moderato, con forza

The Cranes Are Flying

Anton Arensky
1861–1906

Moderato

Salut d'Amour

Edward Elgar
1857–1934

En Bateau

from Petite Suite

Claude Debussy
1862–1918

Andantino

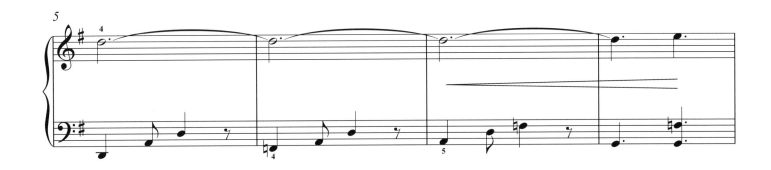

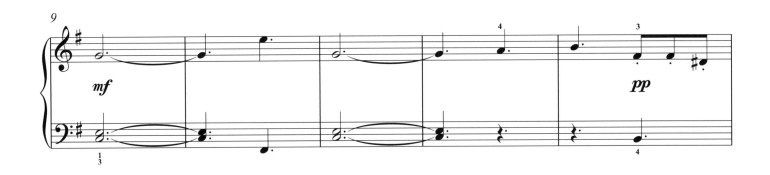

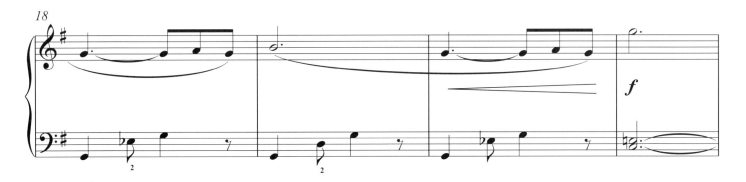

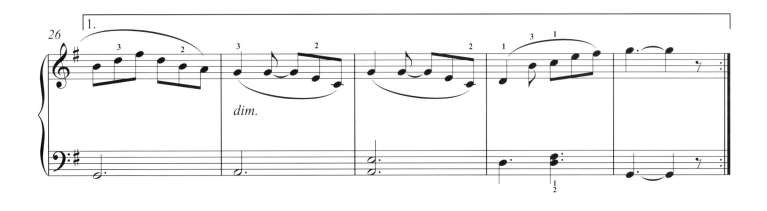

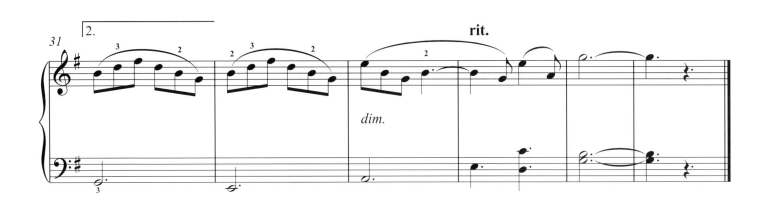

Primavera

No.1 *from* Historiettes

Alexander Gretchaninoff
1864–1956

L'Ombre

No.4 *from* Historiettes

Alexander Gretchaninoff
1864–1956

Promenade au Bois

No.1 *from* Préparatifs pour la Promenade

Alexander Gretchaninoff
1864–1956

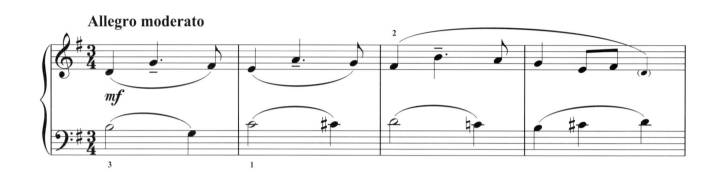

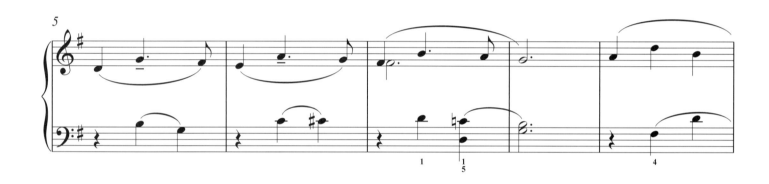

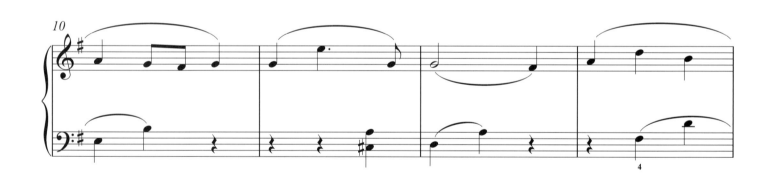

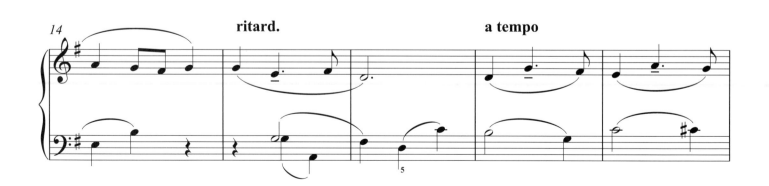

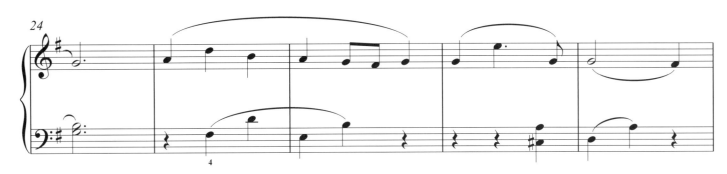

ritard.   a tempo

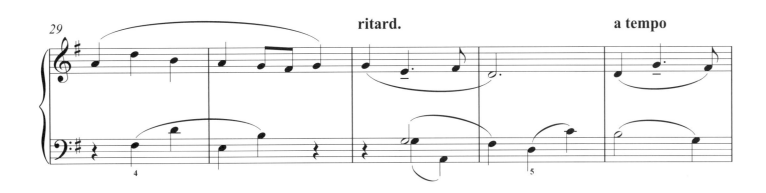

rall.   Meno mosso

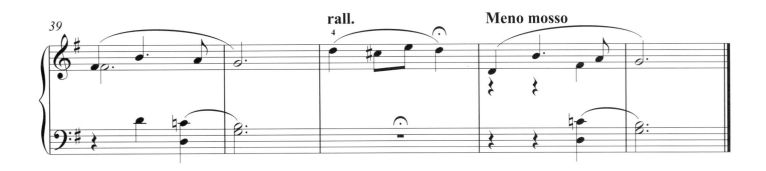

Jupiter

from The Planets

Gustav Holst
1874–1934

Andante maestoso

The Piebald Circus Pony

from Five Pastels, Op.51

Felix Swinstead
1880–1959

Chanson rêveuse de l'Héliotrope

No.9 *from* Pièces d'amour

Reynaldo Hahn
1874–1947

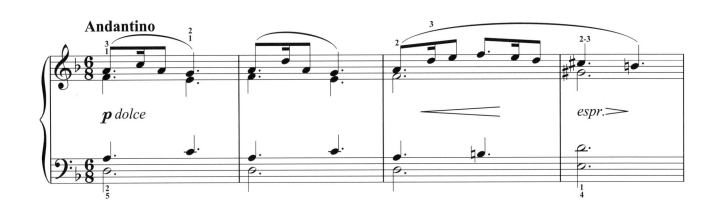

Valse de la Libellule en deuil

No.12 *from* Pièces d'amour

Reynaldo Hahn
1874–1947

La Calinerie

No.3 *from* Cinq Impressions Enfantines

Lucien Wurmser
1877–1967

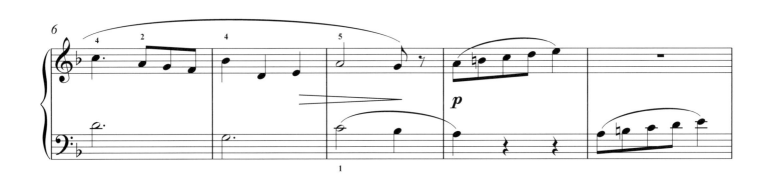

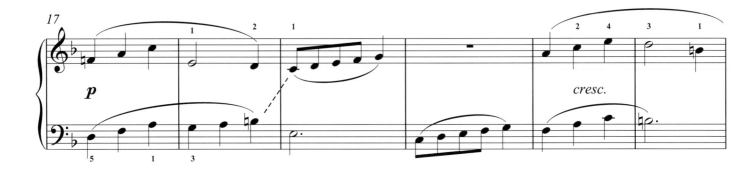

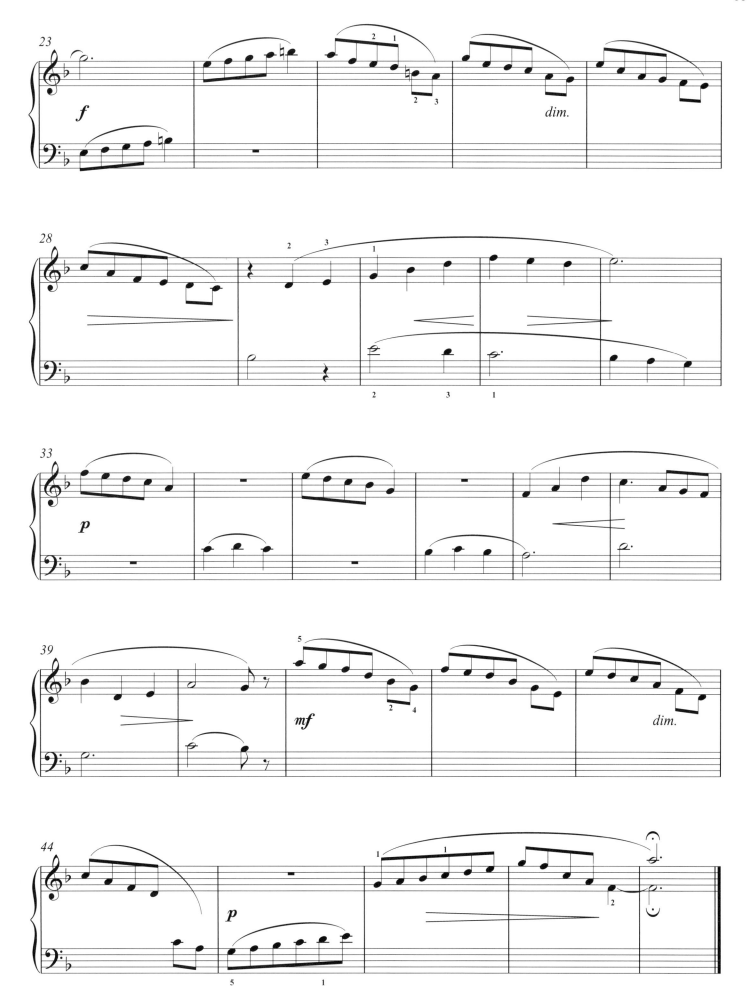

Piano Music For Young And Old

No.2

Carl Nielsen
1865–1931

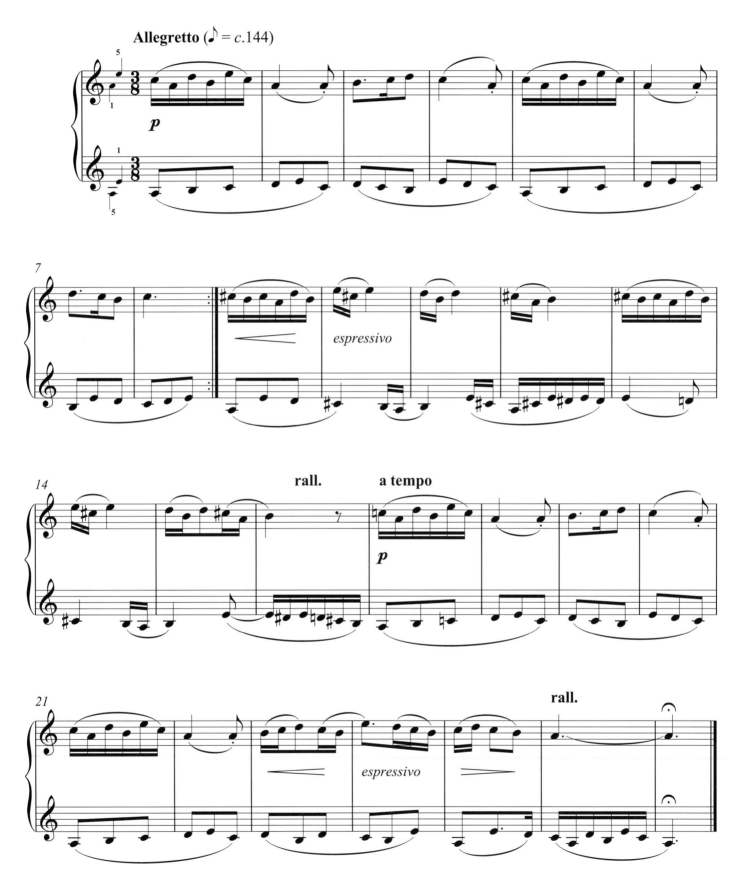

Former Friends

No.3 *from* For Children, Vol.1

Béla Bartók
1881–1945

Children's Song

No.2 *from* For Children, Vol.1

Béla Bartók
1881–1945

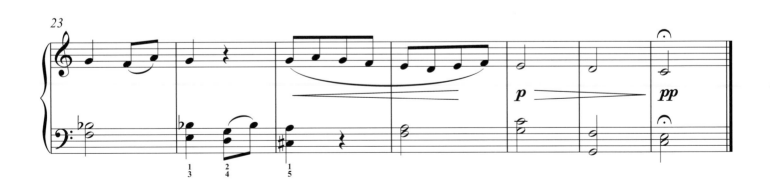

Lento

No.6 *from* Les Cinq Doigts

Igor Stravinsky
1882–1971

Andantino

No.1 *from* Les Cinq Doigts

Igor Stravinsky
1882–1971

Prelude

No.4 *from* Five Miniature Preludes And Fugues

Alec Rowley
1892–1958

Fugue

No.4 *from* Five Miniature Preludes And Fugues

Alec Rowley
1892–1958

Triumphant

from Moods

Iain Kendell
1931–2001

Mythologies Japonaises

No.3

Jehan Alain
1911–1940

Le Dieu Isanagi a jeté son auguste jupe.

Tempo I

Slumber Song

Morton Gould
1913–1996

Like a lullaby

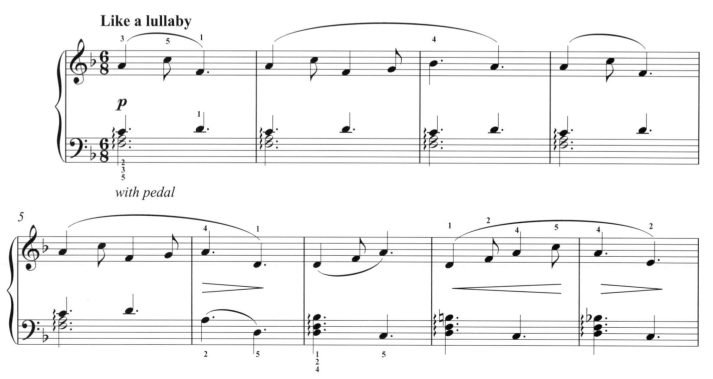

with pedal

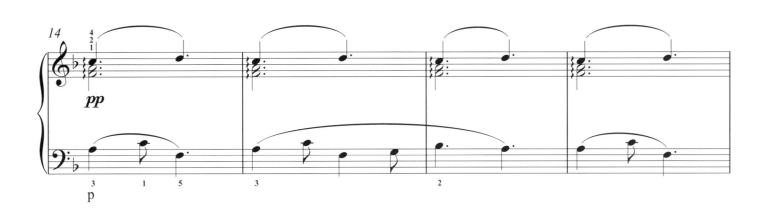

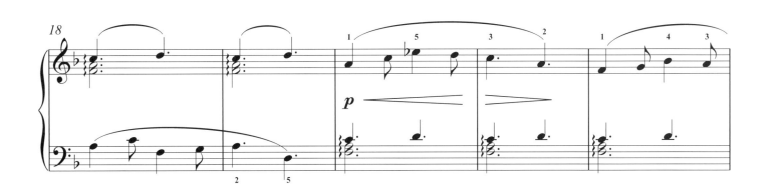

(Sleep,   sleep,   sleep.)

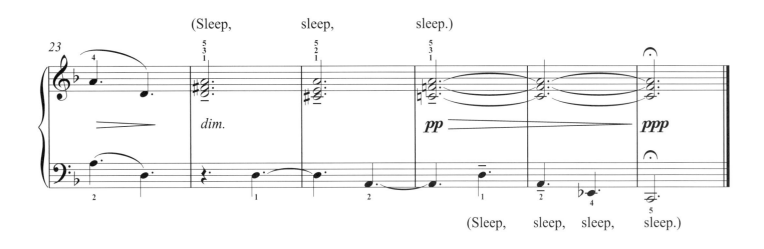

(Sleep,   sleep,   sleep,   sleep.)

The Swan

from Pieces For Angela

Kenneth Leighton
1929–1988

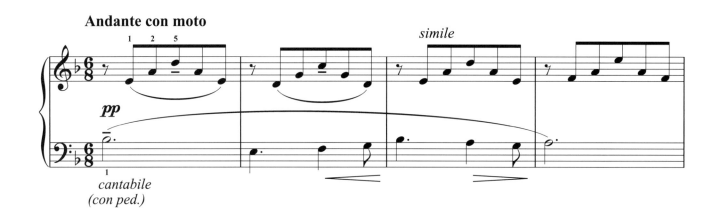

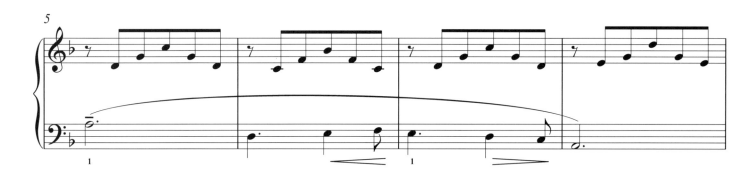

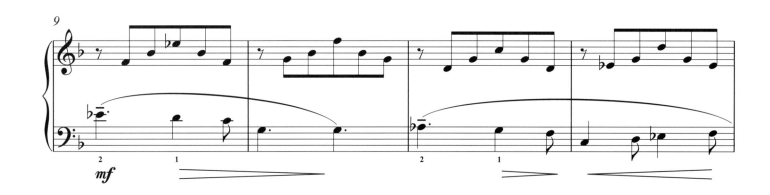

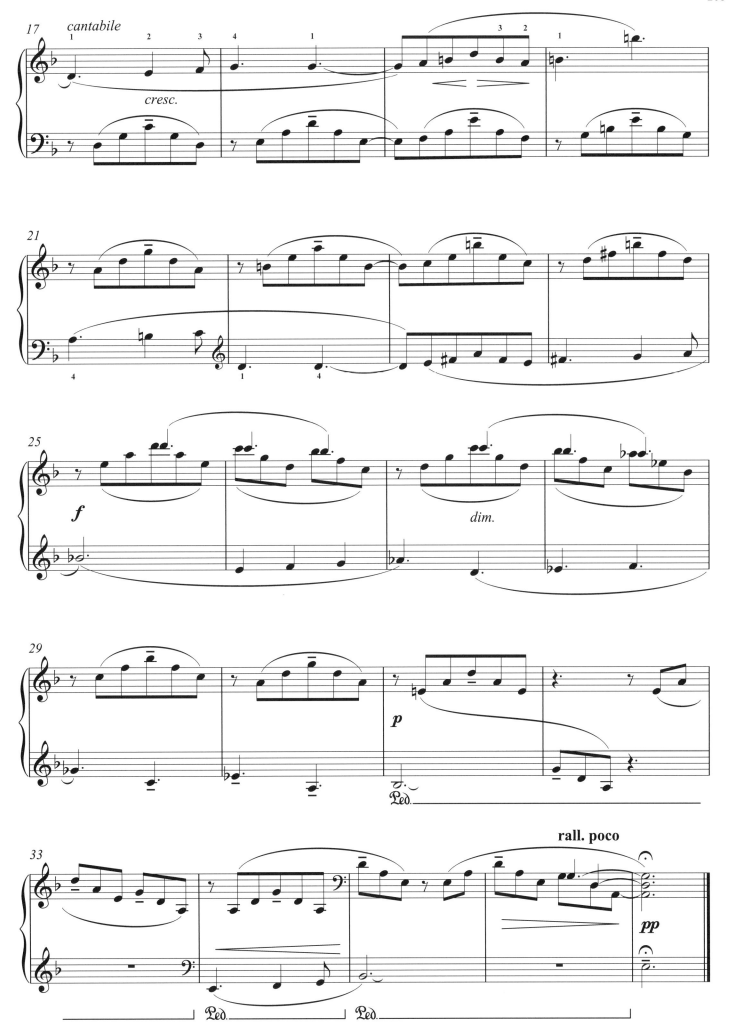

For Erik Satie

No.1 *from* Eight Very Easy Pieces For Piano

Peter Dickinson
b.1934

Just a Waltz

No.8 *from* Eight Very Easy Pieces For Piano

Peter Dickinson
b.1934

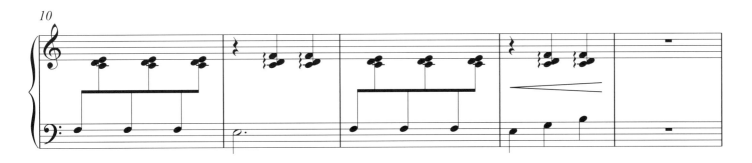

rit.   a tempo

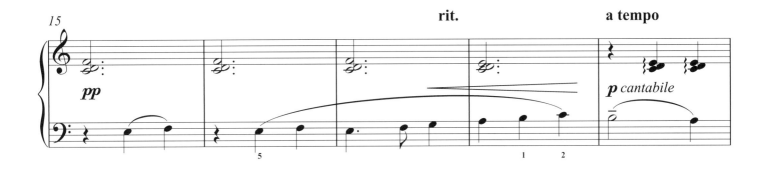

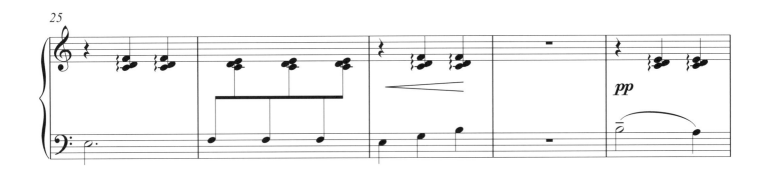

Six Secret Songs

No.1

Peter Maxwell Davies
b.1934

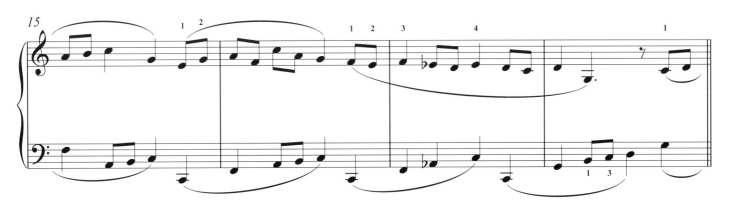

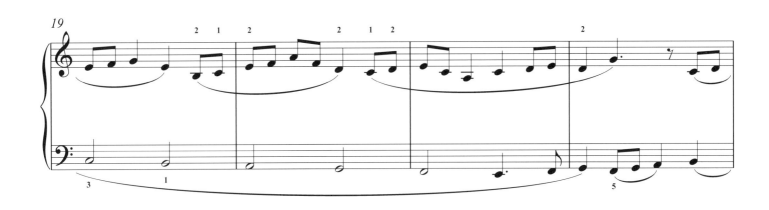

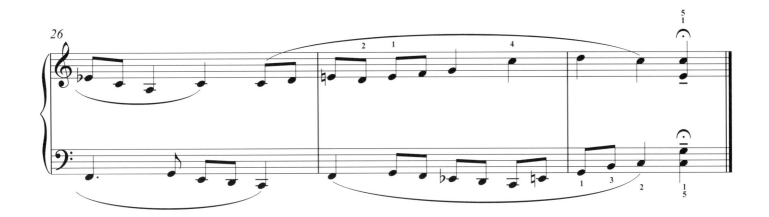

Six Secret Songs

No.2

Peter Maxwell Davies
1934–2016

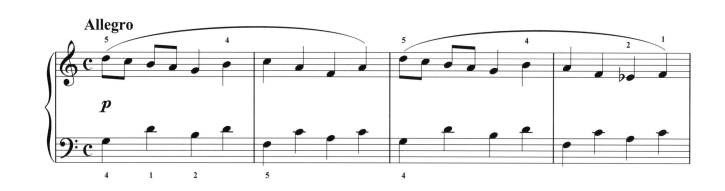

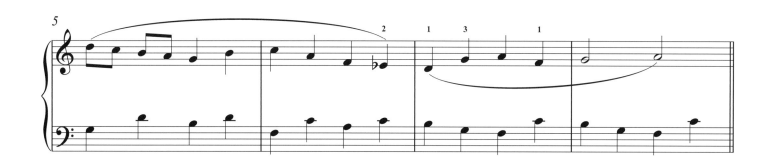

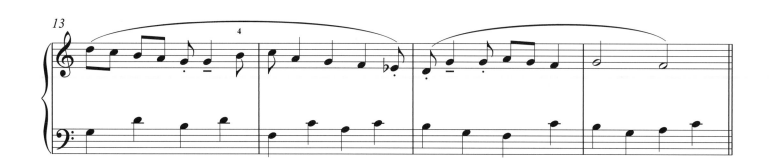

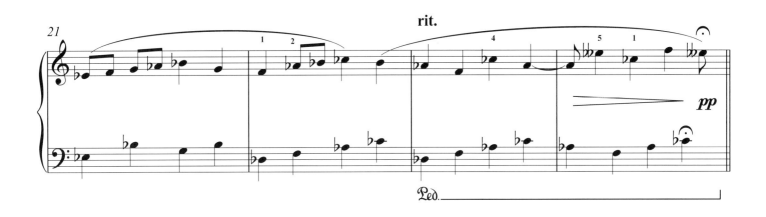

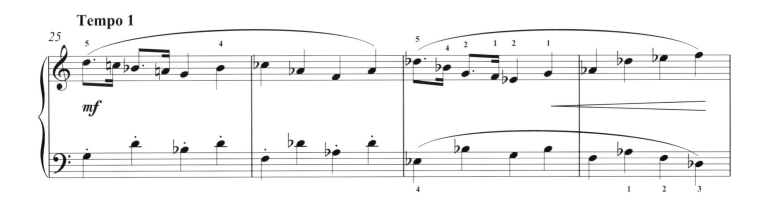

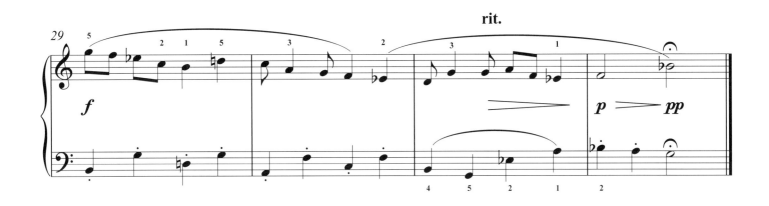

Metamorphosis One

Philip Glass
b.1937

Moderate (♩ = 108–112)

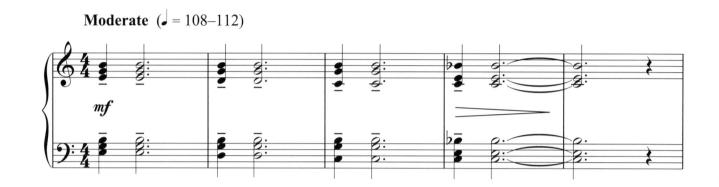

(♩ = 120)

(R.H.)

rit.

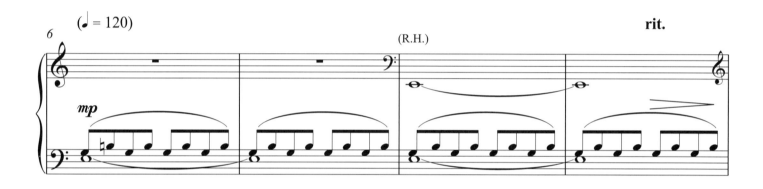

a tempo
(♩ = 108–112)

(♩ = 120)

(R.H.)

rit.

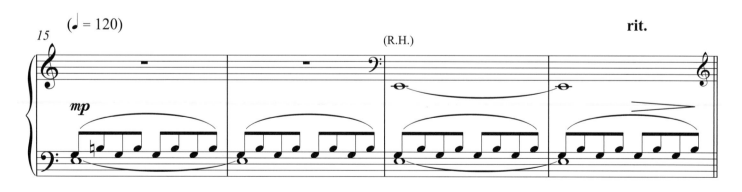

a tempo

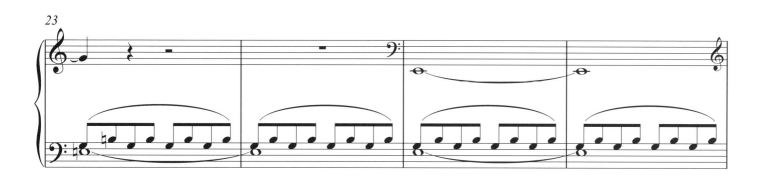

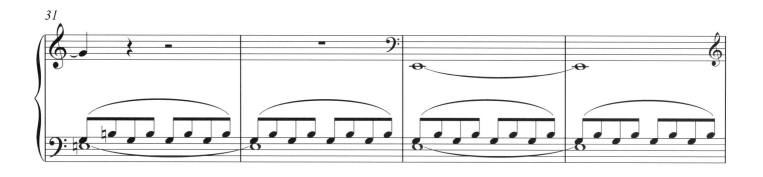

a tempo

1.2.

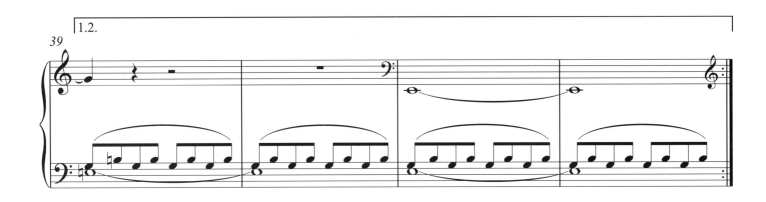

3.

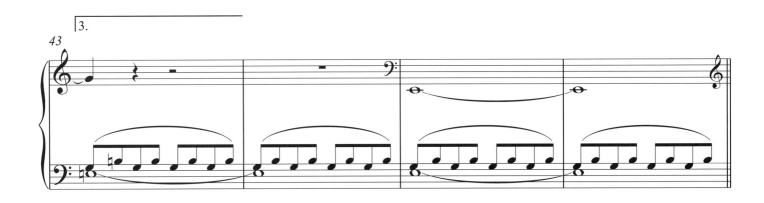

($\quad$ = 108–112)

(♩ = 104)

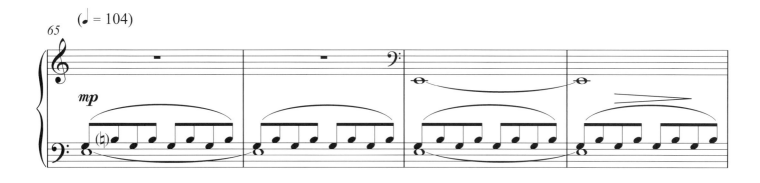

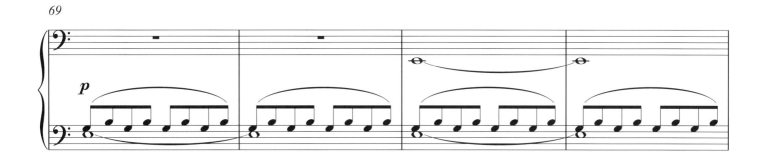

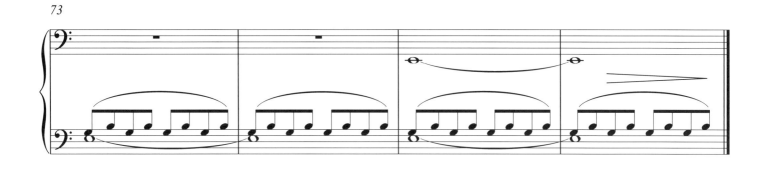

A Sentimental Waltz

from Waiting – Nine Easy Pieces For Piano

Geoffrey Burgon
1941–2010

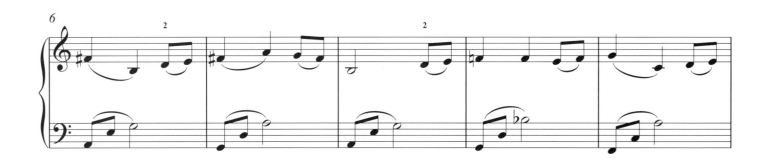

Chatterbox Waltz

Michael Nyman
b.1944

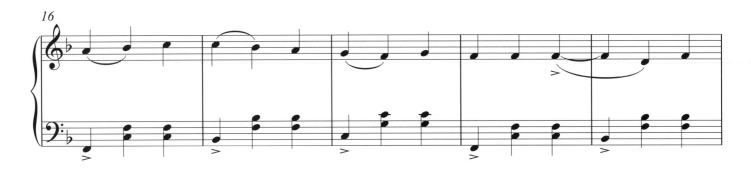

The Exchange

Michael Nyman
b.1944

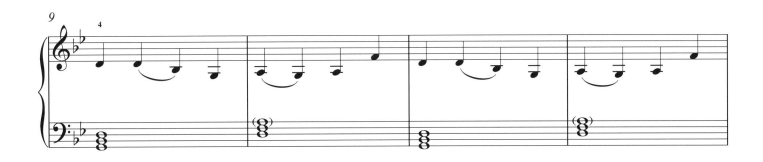

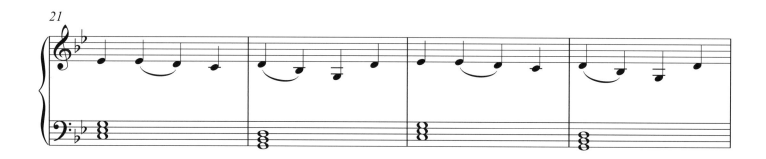

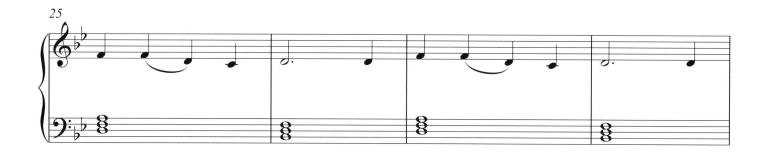

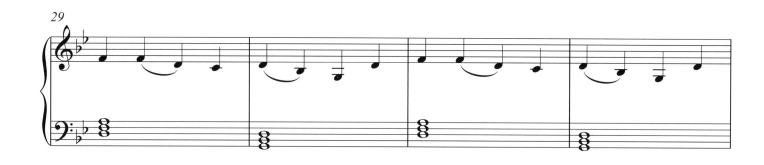

Eleanor Ruth

from In The Pink

Brian Chapple
b.1945

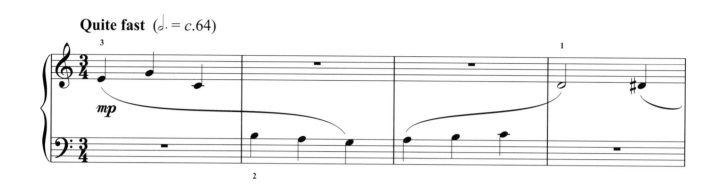

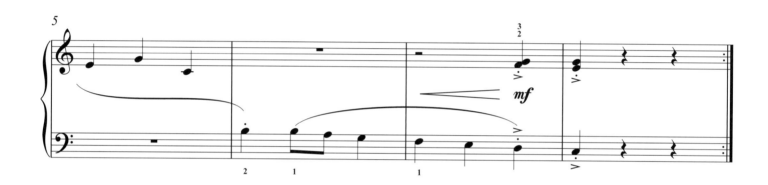

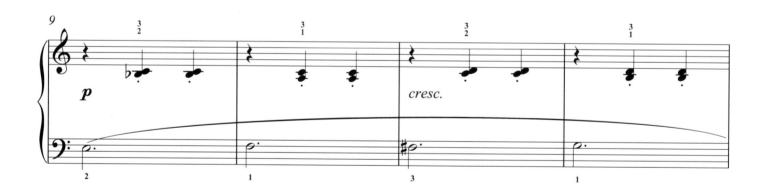

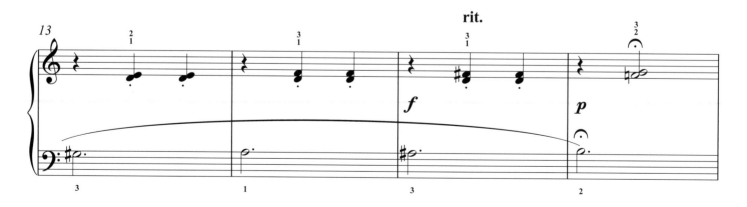

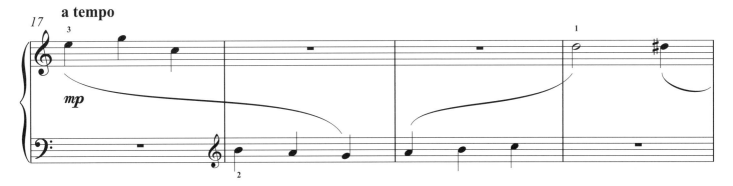

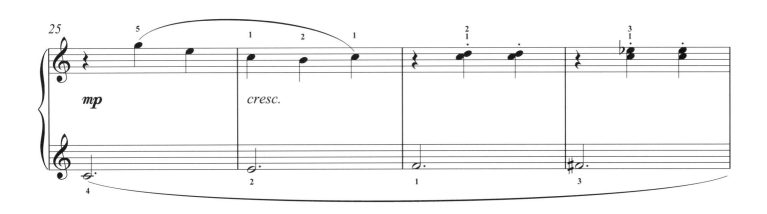

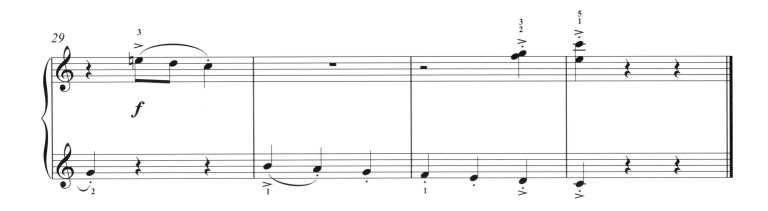

Aria

from Six Tunes For Lucy

Colin Matthews
b.1946

White On White

No.6 *from* Zebra Music

Giles Swayne
b.1946

Black On White

No.12 *from* Zebra Music

Giles Swayne
b.1946

Questa Volta

Ludovico Einaudi
b.1955

134

Sarabande

Ludovico Einaudi
b.1955

138

Three Secrets From The Abyss

No.1

John Harle
b.1956

With quiet simplicity, but intense introspection ♩ = *c.*62

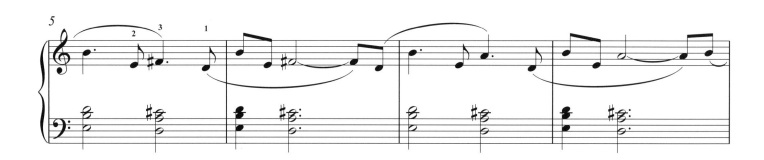

Etude No.1

Jorge Grundman
b.1961

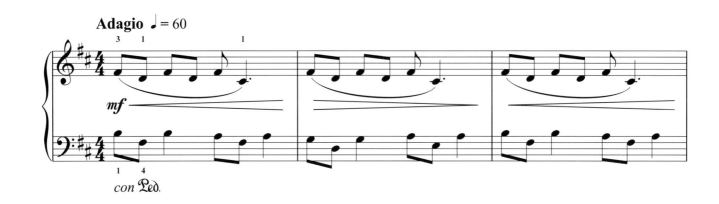

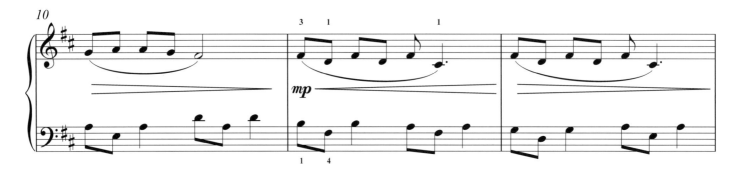

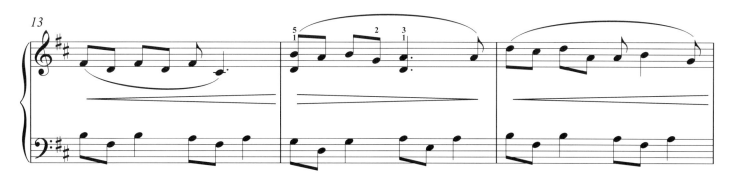

molto rit.

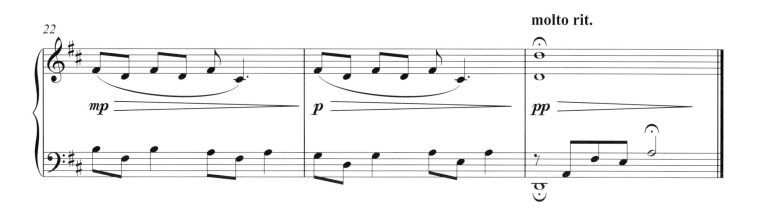

Fragments

Hauschka
b.1966

The Blue Notebooks

Max Richter
b.1966

Pleine Lune

No.3 *from* Les Classiques du Joker

Stéphane Blet
b.1969

2 Years

Neil Cowley
b.1972

Tiger Moth

Neil Cowley
b.1972

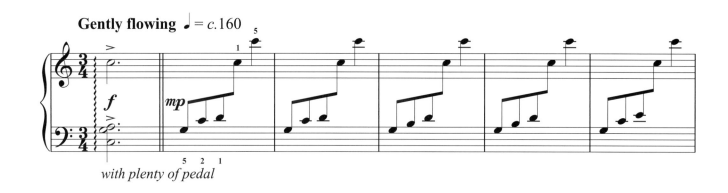

with plenty of pedal

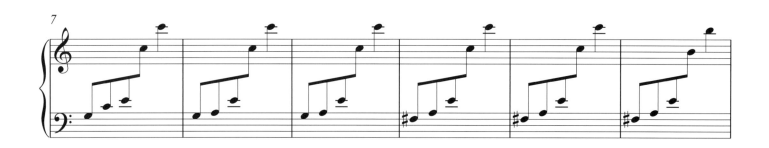

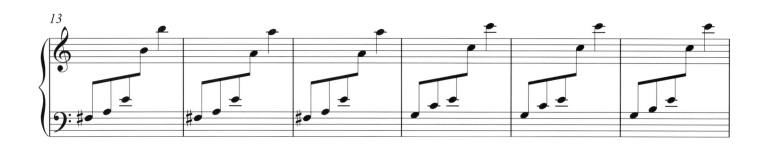

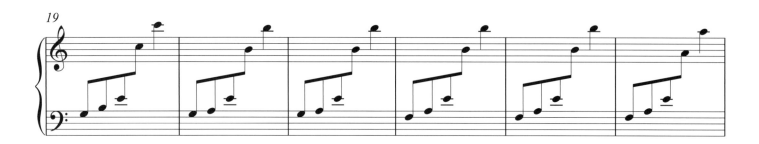

25
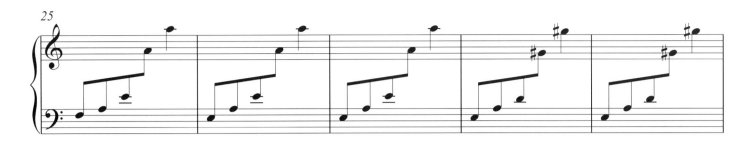

30

35

40

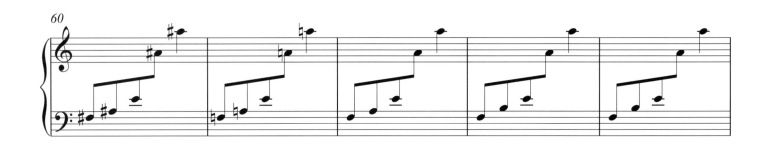

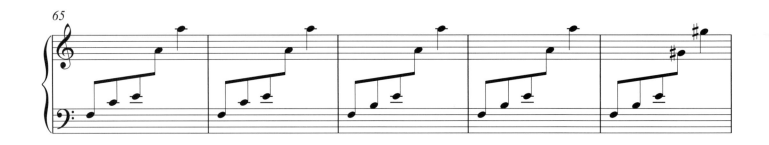

rall...

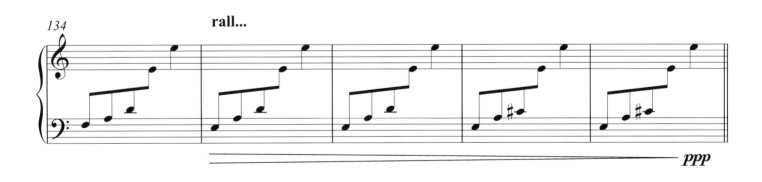

Opus 26

Dustin O'Halloran
b.1971

A walking pace, feel the space

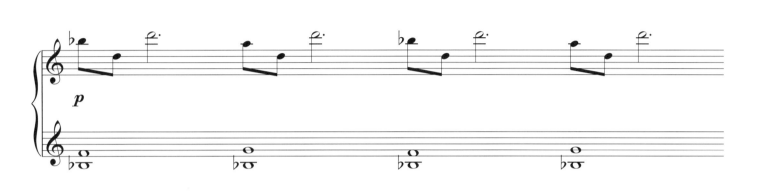

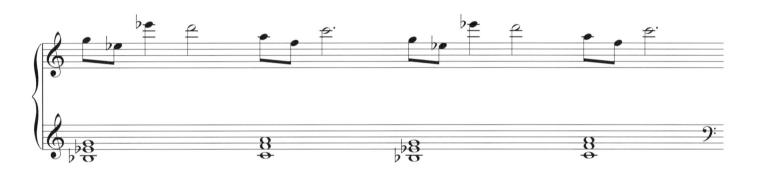

Snowblind

Bowen Liu
b.1983

CLASSICS TO MODERNS

A selection of original piano music as written by the master composers of four centuries. The music provides the pianist with a repertoire which is enjoyable for player and listener alike. Inspired by the popular series by Denes Agay.

New Classics to Moderns
Third series in six books

Book 1 YK22110	Book 4 YK22143
Book 2 YK22121	Book 5 YK22154
Book 3 YK22132	Book 6 YK22165

Each of the six books contains an outstanding selection of original music spanning more than four centuries. A wide representation of composers includes contemporary masters with works from recent decades, as well as lesser known writers whom the performer will be delighted to encounter. Students, teachers, indeed all pianists, will find these pieces a priceless source of study material, recital pieces, sight reading exercises — or just relaxing musical entertainment.

Classics to Moderns
First series in six books

Book 1 YK20014	Book 4 YK20048
Book 2 YK20022	Book 5 YK20055
Book 3 YK20030	Book 6 YK20063

More Classics to Moderns
Second series in six books

Book 1 YK20121	Book 4 YK20154
Book 2 YK20139	Book 5 YK20162
Book 3 YK20147	Book 6 YK20170